My Recommendation

If you have an interest in making money online, recommend something. Because truth is, as an affiliate, you're not necessarily selling anything, you're recommending things.

I don't consider myself a great salesman, the products and the tools that I recommend, seem to sell themselves.

So, think about your life, you go and you recommend things to friends all the time. You recommend restaurants, certain types of foods, movies, cars, products, and all types of different services all the time. Your friends take your recommendations and go check them out for themselves. Some buy, some don't. It's not that you're trying to sell anybody anything.

One of the best programs that I have been making money from is http://www.mylicenserights.com/

And guess what, if it is something that you want to recommend to other people, you can purchase it and earn quite large commissions. I'm talking $1,000+!!

Basically what I'm trying to say is, if you want to make money online, invest in a program, and simply recommend that program to someone else, and that's how you earn money.

You've Got a Video Camera Now Put it to Work

How to Make Money Filming Inexpensive Music Videos

To Emily,

Happy 13th birthday,

enjoy...

From Lisa

xox

It's not about sales, it's not about giving your link out to someone and hoping they're smart enough to take action on it, typically the average person will not.

What you have to do is talk about the concept, and then you say, "let me know if you need a recommendation on where to get this".

Let me give you a quick example, the program that I've invested in where I earn $1000+ commissions. I never talk about the program directly; I only talk about the dozens and dozens if not hundreds of concepts within the program.

And when someone hears that, it's interesting to them, but incomplete.

So people reach out to me and say, "tell me more!"

"How do I get that?" "Where do I find this concept you're talking about"?

So guess what I do? I recommend the program that I'm using to make money online. And, if they want to get in the business, they want to make money, they want to recommend things?

They literally invest in the program and begin duplicating what I did with them, guiding their prospect down the path, it's very easy to do.

So, invest in a program that you can recommend to people that will pay you commissions.

I recommend you start HERE>>>> http://www.mylicenserights.com/

Table of Contents

1. Introduction

Man has always been mesmerized by the world around him and has always tried to capture things that fascinated him in a single frame. From the Neanderthals in the caves, painting mammoths and stick figures with spears, all the way to the modern Homo Sapiens with machines that can make pictures with a millimeter precise resolution. All of that because of mankinds need to immortalize and record various events that evolve around him.

The invention of the camera revolutionized society because it gave Man the power to visualize memories, categorize history and even stop time for that millisecond the flash comes. With this newfound technology, a new branch of art was created, a branch called photography and from it, an even more stunning discipline emerged, cinematography. Stories from books didn't have to be imagined through reading anymore, now, they could be seen and heard. As it rose, so did the media and it grows more powerful with each and every photograph taken or video created.

This will serve as some sort of a tutorial for all you who are willing to dive into the massive ocean of media and multimedia and with some luck and a great deal of skill, emerge from it victorious.

2. Ways to make money filming inexpensive music videos

I'm not going to beat around the bush here since we both know why you're reading this. You want to take a bite out of the music industry's diamond mine, or to put it simply, you're here to make money. Now, I'm not going to tell you that you need this and that before telling you if it's worth it. And to answer that question right away, yes, it's worth it. Sure, it takes a no small amount of effort and a lot of time spent on pondering if this was a good idea or not but trust me, it gets real good when you break the ice. Also, don't roll your eyes every time you see 'effort' because nothing in this world falls out of the sky.

Success isn't built on wishes; it's built on hard work fueled by an indomitable will. So before wasting your time any more by reading this, ask yourself do YOU want to succeed and how bad do you want it? Are you willing to wake up early every morning to take a perfect picture of the sun rising? Are you willing to stay up late editing your video to perfection? Go ahead, ask yourself. Take your time; this is a big decision after all.

Done? Good. If you've continued reading this then I presume (and hope) that your answer is yes. Let me be the first to welcome you here. Just take a number and stand in line with the other thousands of people who are determined just like you are. Thousands you ask? You didn't think that you were the only one, did you? If you did, man, you're in for a big surprise. It's a huge world out there and each and every person wants to succeed, wants to be remembered for something and all of them are in one big race that pretty much has no finish line. Either you're in it or you're not.

How to make yourself stand out then? Be innovative. "That's not so simple." Or is it? Write down the first thing that pops to your mind and try searching it on the web. Chances are that only a few or maybe even none have come up with the same idea that you have. The point is, don't just follow the main line. Go off road for a bit. Every great mind in history was 'unique' in its own way and has changed the way we see the world. Why? Because they saw it differently and they showed the rest how they saw it. Don't be afraid to stand out. Alright, I think I rambled on long enough about motivation and success.

Now I'll tell you how and where to make money while spending little to none. There are numerous things you can film that can bring you some profit. Some of them may seem miniscule to you but hell, you have to start somewhere.

There are thousands of bands out there that are yet to be noticed in this world. In order to make themselves more known and popular, they need music videos and that's where you come in. Find a fresh local band that wants to be famous (they all do) and ask them. I'm sure that they would be thrilled to get their own video. Now, the rewards here aren't really that high, they're actually the bare minimum of something you could call 'profit', but it's a start and soon enough, you'll be signing contracts with big rock and pop stars out there.

Concerts-Yes, concerts. Not all concerts get full time coverage by the media. There are a lot of bands that start out doing small gigs in night clubs and pubs. Some bands appear on the stage for only one song but still, no matter where they are, they want it covered. A word of advice, plan ahead. When you get the job of covering a gig or concert, don't just stand there and wait for the day to come. Plan it out. You have the time, date and location where the gig/concert will take place. Go to that place a few days before it starts and scout out the area.

Where is the best angle? Where is the best lightning? Where to position my camera? Those are all questions that you can answer when you get there and when you got it all figured out, it will be much easier to film it when the real deal comes and you'll give your client a high quality video of their performance. Why is quality important? Isn't that obvious? Word gets around. If you put out extra effort out there, it won't go unnoticed. When you rise a bit in reputation, bands will come to YOU to film their performance.

3. Creative tips and tricks

Here I will point out some tips and tricks to make your life easier once you start your business. All of these were collected through trial and error. There's no easy way out, you know? You have to hit the ground a few times to learn your lesson but that's where tips come in. They don't erase your ability to fail, they just help you lower the number of times you'll hit the ground. Like I said, all of these were collected through trial and error. Others that have come before you have learned these the hard way and were good enough to share their insight with the rest.

Get resourceful-Take a piece of paper and a pen and get to brainstorming. Think about what you have and think about how to use it. Every piece of equipment is valuable and can be used for something.

Decide on a realistic budget-Be honest with yourself. How much can you really afford to spend on your music video? Borrowing equipment, using a free location, doing your own post production or getting a friend to do it for you, will only get you so far. It will still cost a few hundred dollars to make your own music video. Choose a style for your video that fits your band and is affordable.

Crew-If you are making your video on a low budget it is entirely possible your crew will be friends and family of the band. That being the case, they need to understand the fundamentals of what you are trying to do, and essentially, how to operate the equipment they will be using. Make sure you review what you shoot again and again.

On a good note, friends and family are not likely to ask for money, and they are likely to be motivated to help you create as good a video as you possibly can.

Videographer-These guys are a must for the music video industry. And they're expensive. Yeah, they're expensive as hell. Most bands don't have the money to hire professional video production companies or even those budget-rate firms. I mean, it's expensive for a good reason. Even a tiny bit of production requires a LOT of work. The advice here is; cozy up to one. Yes, the advice is simple as that. What did you expect? Those Ancient Chinese prophecies or something? If it's simple, it doesn't mean it isn't important. Knowing the right people can make a big difference in any field of business, cinematography is no exception. You probably already know someone who has a knack for technology; you just have to ask around. Being on good terms with someone with the technical know-how will save you a lot of money and time (and nerves).

Storyboard-I know you may be overwhelmed by the idea of drawing it all out but trust me on this one; it makes things a lot easier. You might have the idea in mind of how you would want it to look like but if you just go and try filming it without storyboarding it first, it's going to turn out messy. And that's not what you want, right? It isn't really that hard when you start doing it and you'll see the fruits of it right away. Not only does the video look better and more fluent, it also makes the editing part a lot easier when you have the things you want written down in front of you. So, grab a piece of paper, a pencil and start pouring your ideas onto it.

The structure of the video should match the structure of the song, meaning, you can use the song's lyrics as sort of guidelines when storyboarding. You might think of it as a big chore but it really isn't when you think about it. When you divide it properly, it doesn't seem that big at all. Those fellas that storyboard movies don't do it whole right away, they go frame by frame and that makes it more digestible. In your case, songs aren't that long, maybe three or four minutes on average so there isn't really much storyboarding to be done. Like I said before, use the lyrics.

For example, the first verse will be here and like this, the bridge here, the chorus here, etc. You get it. Include enough to keep it interesting, but not so much that your video is manic. Simply changing locations is enough to add visual variety. Pop in some wide shots, some medium shots and a few close-ups and voila, there you go! It's great if you have a good and extensive idea for the storyline of the video but keep it down a notch. You want people to like it and share it when they see it, not ask themselves questions such as "What the hell did I just watch?" You know? Just remember, keep it simple.

Backups-I really don't know why I have to mention this at all but I'll say it just in case you didn't get the memo. Make a habit of creating copies of everything you do for your current project. Backups on the hard drive, copies on a USB stick, whatever, just make sure your work is safe. You don't want to come back from the store one day and see that the file got corrupted or your computer broke down. Backups will save you a lot of time and nerves.

Find videos you like and try to recreate what you like about them with your own twist-Keep in mind, I'm not telling you to copy the video completely. I'm just saying that you take the parts that you like and modify them to what you think is good. Maybe you like the close up and background in one video, take that, find a similar background and play around with different camera pans and views. You can even add some new effects to it, maybe a slow motion part when it closes up on the singer's face or something like that. There are millions of music videos out there, if you run out of ideas, just go online and find an inspiration in one of them.

Try to only film exactly what you need, the more you film, the more you have to edit-"The more, the merrier" doesn't quite apply to this business. Excess footage might be nice because you have a wider variety of things to use but it's also a waste of time, resources and disk space. Plan it out, storyboard it and stick to it. That way you'll have everything you need without doing unnecessary extra work.

Effects-I'm not telling you to Photoshop in a space shuttle or something. Keep it simple but keep it creative. If it's a happy song or something with a cheerful rhythm, try to match up the effects to it. For example, if you're shooting the band and the background is a graffiti wall, you can try to make the graffiti come alive if you understand what I mean. You can also post a few song lyrics in the video and time them to appear when the singer sings them. You just have to play around with it. Unleash your imagination and transfer your ideas to the frame.

Props-Stage props aren't really necessary in most videos but there are some bands that do have a specific 'style' to them and will ask you about some props for the videos. Don't buy the props, ever. Rent them out or even-make them yourself. Everything around you can be used as a prop, it just needs a little touch ups here and there and it's good to go.

Be happy-Yeah, it's a weird one again. But believe me, it's a crucial one. Have fun! You're doing this job because it's interesting to you and you want to do it so you should have fun anyway. Talk a lot on breaks, crack jokes, and bring snacks, anything to keep people around you smiling. Why? Hours of shooting something can make anyone a bit tense and edgy and just being nice can help lift up the atmosphere a lot. Moreover, if the band you're shooting is happy and is having fun, they'll appear more natural on the tape. And that can go a long way. So, smile! :)

4. Deciding on locations

Picking out the perfect location for your shooting is indeed very important, it has to suit the song and band, it has to be free of distractions and it has to be visually appealing. When you start your project with the band, take your time to listen to the song they want in the video and analyze the lyrics. While this may sound like an unnecessary step, it will help you a lot in picking out the suitable location. If it's a love song with a happy beat, you aren't going to shoot it in a rundown building, right? You're going to find a place with a lot of light, lot of color and positive energy, like a meadow or a graffiti wall or something like that. Anyway, you get the point I'm trying to make. Humans are primarily visual beings and if what they see is appealing to them, chances are that they are going to like the song a lot more than if it were unappealing. Remember when I mentioned planning ahead? That also applies for this one.

Don't pick out too many locations too. It will be a problem moving around locations every few shots. You can also do everything in just one location, the visual variety being that each frame has the band in another angle or another position. The possibilities are endless. You'll just have to experiment a bit with this one. Just follow your gut and it will all work out just fine.

5. Renting inexpensive equipment for video shoot

Alright, we've covered how to make money, some tips and advice, locations and now onto the equipment you'll need. All you need to get started is a camera and a few additional accessories; a tripod, a microphone and a computer with an editing software. You can even skip all that and film and edit on your iPhone or iPad. In the beginning, don't spend too much on gear, just buy basic things. Also buy clever. Don't buy things you'll only use a few times, you can rent those. Don't spend your entire budget on a camera; don't spend even half on it. It really isn't necessary. Besides, you need to buy other stuff like sound recording gear, lenses and other kit. A DSLR or mirrorless camera is the most affordable way to get good quality images. I think the Canon 700D/T5i is the best entry-level camera for low budget filmmaking.

Sound recording

If your camera has the right sockets, you can get much better sounds by using a separate microphone. If you don't have this option, you can create soundtracks on your computer as you edit. You might spend a little extra on a good microphone. There will be a lot more background noise but the sound will be clearer and more audible than with a lousy microphone. The background noise can be edited out.

Supporting and moving the camera around

You need to be able to keep your camera firm and steady while you move it and assuming that you're not a brain surgeon or something, your hands are probably shaky. You don't want to spend a few hours taking pictures or filming only to notice that the image is blurry or hazy. The solution? You need a tripod. It will make your life a whole lot easier. You can also get monopods, tracking systems, stabilizers (to 'fly' the camera) and cranes but all in due time. The tripod is quite enough for a beginner.

Lightning

Lightning is just as important as having a camera. Even a state of the art camera can fall victim to bad lightning. Sure, we have automated light adjustments on those cameras but since this is for making videos on a budget, I'll leave out the NASA stuff. Don't buy film lights unless it's absolutely necessary, even then, it's better to rent them out than buy them. Those things are expensive and awkward to carry. You can buy professional lighting in sets, either as tungsten lights ('redheads') or as cold LED lights. LED lights are more expensive and cooler; LED 'arrays' are good for producing even, soft lighting. You can get 'soft boxes' to produce this kind of lighting with tungsten lights. For enhancing natural light, get a cheap five in one reflector, which includes a diffuser (to reduce and soften light); gold, white and silver reflectors (for filling shadows); and a black side to use as a 'flag' (to block out light). A short tip; you can also use builders' work lights or high powered torches instead of pro lights. They work just fine.

Editing software

Editing software is just as important as the rest of the equipment. It will help you achieve the special effects you can't normally do with a camera. You can get free editing software for your Mac's and PC's but if you want something better and more extensive, you'll have to buy the professional editions. Some examples are Apple's Final Cut Pro X or Adobe Premiere Pro. I would suggest you buy a laptop but before you do that, evaluate whether you really need one. If you don't need something portable, it's much better if you invested your money in a desktop computer. Laptop's only advantage is its portability, nothing else. The desktop computer beats the laptop in terms of durability, money and practicality. For example, if some part of your laptop breaks down, it's likely that you won't be able to fix it. If you can fix it, it will be tremendously costly unlike the desktop computer where if something breaks down, you just replace it.

Storage

If you're doing some smaller projects, feel free to store all of your data on your main computer (don't forget backups!), but if you're working on something huge and ambitious, you might consider buying an external hard drive. Not only does that prevent your data from being erased and/or corrupted if something goes terribly wrong on your computer, but it also makes you more at ease to know that all your hard work is in safe hands so to speak. Be sure to buy a fast one too. With fast hard drives, smaller drives (for example, 500GB) are said to be more reliable than larger ones. So, weigh out your options and get to it. But remember, be rigorous about making backups.

Video formats

As technology advanced, so did the quality of the photos and videos. Most camcorders today shoot high definition videos, also known as 1080p. There are also ultra-high definition cameras, 4k, which you don't need unless you're a serious professional filmmaker and your film will be shown on really big screens. (Higher resolution video takes up more memory and needs more powerful computers for editing). Remember when the biggest quality you could get was 240p or 144p? Cinematography and photography sure have come a long way since then. But if you can afford it, it may be worth using a camera that shoots higher resolution footage than the film you're making. It means you can crop the footage in the editing software, turning a mid-shot into a close-up or eliminating distracting parts of the picture.

All in all, don't get obsessed over getting the newest gear and all that. Everything doesn't have to be brand new. I told you already, rent, buy used, borrow, anything will work. For a beginner, older equipment is gold. Also make sure you don't become too dependent on your gear. Remember, your ideas are what are in the picture; a camera is just a tool. Ideas, not gear, are the most important things filmmakers need.

6. Types of inexpensive HD video cameras and video editing equipment

There are lots of different kinds of cameras you can use for filmmaking. I'm going to show you cameras that low-budget filmmakers might afford to buy or rent. Like I mentioned earlier, I'm going to put aside the NASA stuff and keep it simple. The majority has agreed that for them, a DSLR or mirrorless camera, gives the best results in image quality for that price and it doesn't matter if you're an amateur or a professional in this business. If you want to go a step further, an interchangeable lend camera gives you the best of a DSLR with even better image quality and comfort in handling. Action cameras are great if you're going to add a bit of rapid movement to your shoot.

DSLRs and mirrorless cameras:

Still cameras with interchangeable lenses are the cheapest way to shoot really good quality video. For beginners, I would recommend the Canon T5i/700D and the mirrorless EOS-M. Professionals will want something like the mirrorless Panasonic GH3GH4 or the full frame 5d MkIII.

Pros-Good when there's a shortage of light, good focus effects, lots of creative control.

Cons-Sound recording is a bit tricky, limited recording time, weird to handhold; you might have some small image quality problems here and there.

Prosumer camcorders:

The Canon XA20 and similar cameras like it have a better image and sound quality than consumer camcorders. They give you more control of it and you'll get better results in places where there's a shortage of light. Most prosumer cameras have ports for microphones and headphones, although they lack the features of a pro camera.

Pros-Fairly good image and sound quality, they're easy to use and better to handle than the DSLRs.

Cons-It's a lot bigger than most camcorders, image quality may not be accepted by broadcasters and they're not as good as system still cameras.

Pro camcorders:

Pro camcorders give you a lot more control than other basic or prosumer camcorders. Most of them will let you plug in pro microphones. The majority of the controls are dials and buttons rather than menus. This lets you can work faster once you're used to the camera. Buy these only if you're into some serious filmmaking, they shoot in ultra-high definition (4k) but they're expensive.

Pros-Fairly good image and sound quality, lots of control, they're quick to use once you get familiar with them.

Cons-Expensive, takes some time to learn and they can be a bit bulky.

Interchangeable lens video cameras:

These cameras have the best features of both pro camcorders and system still cameras. The big sensors and interchangeable lenses make for really good image quality. Most of them also have professional sound features, are easier to handle than DSLR's, and record in formats that stand up better to being manipulated when you start editing them than basic DSLR footage. They don't suffer the 'moiré' effect. Like with the pro camcorders above, buy these only if you're in for something serious, otherwise they aren't necessary.

Pros-Great image quality, good when there's a shortage of light and lots of creative control.

Cons-They're expensive and most of them are quite big.

Consumer camcorders:

These are the pretty much regular cameras that you see everywhere. They're quite affordable and aren't really that bad. These are pretty good for a starter, you can buy something better when you can afford it but meanwhile, these will do the trick. They're easier to film and handle with than iPads and have reasonably good built-in microphones.

Pros-They're small and easy to handle, good and simple controls, they usually have better image stabilization than the DSLRs.

Cons-Image and sound isn't as good as prosumer or pro cameras, especially in shortage of light.

Smartphones and tablets:

Yes, they're also an option. Sure, they are plain but they're not as bad as you think they are. You can shoot and then edit your video on iPads and iPhones. With the right apps, they can be quite useful if you need something shot quickly. Also, they're simple to use.

Pros-They're very easy to use, you can take them anywhere and there isn't a problem with transportation since they mostly fit in your pocket and you can shoot and edit on one device which is pretty neat when you come to think of it.

Cons-Sound and image quality won't be as good as a video camera, particularly in some difficult situations and conditions. Also, tablets are weird to hold.

Compact still cameras:

A lot of these cameras can shoot HD video. But if you're buying a camera specifically for filmmaking, you're probably better off getting a camcorder or DSLR.

Pros-They're small and they won't get in the way of anything, easy to handle.

Cons-Sound quality won't be good and they probably lack a port for an external microphone. These are more suited for discreet filming and such.

Action cameras:

These little cameras are like the Hulk from the Avengers, except the size. You wouldn't want to use one as your main camera but they're tough and can go through a lot before breaking. You can mount them on pretty much everything. Most of them don't have screens so you have no idea what you're shooting, although you can get a more expensive one that lets you monitor the image with a wireless monitor.

Pros-They're small and tough as nails.

Cons-No viewfinder and it's just basic sound.

Now, after reading all of this, you might ask why did I even mention all of these, why didn't I tell you the best one for filming music videos and got it over with? The reason why is fairly simple. There is no complete answer to those questions. You buy the type that you need the most and you rent out the others. Different bands will have different requests and you'll have to improvise a lot. But regardless of what type you use, make sure that they fulfil the following points.

Ease of use:

This one's a must of course. Filming for a few hours can be quite uncomfortable even with a right camera, why make it worse by picking out something that looks like a hedgehog? Is it comfortable to hold? Is it easy to use? Are the controls hard? Is there a port for a microphone or a light in the camera? All of these matter.

Manual control:

Can you set the options like exposure and white-balance yourself? These don't sound important right now, but later on when you get serious about it, they will come in handy.

Lens:

How far does the camera zoom out or zoom in? The wide-angle setting is probably more important as it lets you get close and makes handholding quite easier. Forget about the digital zoom, it's the optical zoom range that you really need.

Sound:

Some cameras have a built-in microphone and some don't. For those that do, check if it's good or not. For those that don't, check the camera for any ports. Most cameras have ports for external microphones.

Image stabilization:

Not necessary if you're using a tripod or something else to stabilize the image, although it's quite useful when you're handholding it. It makes the image less shaky.

Sensor size:

Size doesn't matter here. If it's bigger, it doesn't mean it's better. At least not for what you're doing. You always need to weigh your options and discern between what you need and what you don't need.

Recording format:

You have to pay attention to everything, including the format and file size (some would even say 'especially the format and file size') because some editing programs don't support some file formats and you don't want to be in the situation where you film it and then realize that it can't open the file. You can try to convert the file but that has its own dose of risk. The image and sound quality of the video can suffer tremendously but the worst case scenario would be that the file gets corrupted.

And now I'll tell you which things to ignore. Don't let them fool you into thinking that it's better than something else. Be clever about it.

Special effects:

You have editing software. Why in the hell would you need special effects on a camera then? Any effects you want, just edit them in later.

Digital zoom:

Digital zoom sounds fancy and the way they promote it makes it seem like it's the best thing in the world. But it's not. It's just a way of electronically zooming into the picture, which is quite low quality. Only the optical zoom counts.

Megapixels:

Don't let them fool you on this one. More megapixels doesn't mean better, especially in this business since it can make the image quality quite bad when there's a shortage of light. More megapixels are better for big prints, not for filmmaking.

7. Green screens

What is a green screen? It is when you replace the real background of a video with a digital one. To put it simply, it offers the most natural-looking way to integrate a human with other types of content you might want to show, such as presentation slides, screen video, screenshots, photos or animated elements. It also gives you a new way to save money. Instead of buying fancy props or renting out a studio, the green screen can give your video an expensive looking aesthetic. You can replace the background with anything you want or need. To start shooting with it, you just need a regular digital camera, some editing software and a wall that doesn't have any color that appears on the people in the frame (clothes, skin, hair, etc.).

Since finding a wall like that is extremely hard, you'll be better off with buying a piece of muslin cloth that's a hideous shade of green. That way you make sure that anything else in the frame doesn't interfere with the digital and graphical part of the green screen. Regarding the camera, I suggest buying a camera that can shoot high definition videos. That makes it easier to import the file while editing and all that. Although lightning can be a problem because of the background shadows, those can be edited out with a few extra minutes of your time. But if you're having trouble getting the background to fully disappear or there's a slight halo around the person, it means you need to upgrade your lighting.

The more even your lighting, the better the effect will be. Aim the lights so that the green screen doesn't have dark areas and bright areas. Focus your efforts on the area directly behind the person, as you'll be able to crop out the excess space around the person later (don't forget to factor in the person's "gesture zone"). When you're buying the lights, look for "continuous lighting"–as opposed to flash or strobe lighting. It's much better at giving you what you want than other types.

8. Bartering

Bartering is a system of exchange by which goods or services are directly exchanged for other goods or services without using a medium of exchange, such as money. That's what Wikipedia says anyway. But it's pretty much it. For example, you want something edited and your friend (who knows how to edit) wants something shot, you strike a deal, you will shoot something for him while he edits your video (It's a stupid example but nothing better came up, it serves its purpose so stop complaining).

While bartering may sound like an ancient form of trade, it is actually quite efficient, especially for us who work on a budget. When you start working as a filmmaker, it won't be long before you stumble upon other people who are just like you. You'll probably meet the majority of your 'colleagues' on forums. There are special forums devoted completely to cinematography and photography. There you'll find pretty useful tips from others on locations, ideas, bands etc. As you meet more people, the option of bartering won't seem silly anymore.

You've got something I need and I've got something you need. We meet, discuss it a bit and voila, you got what you need and I've got what I need and everyone's happy!

9. Where to promote your business?

This is pretty much the same as with camera types. There is no absolute answer. I mean, I could tell you to promote it in every way possible, which isn't a bad idea at all, but in order to conserve money and time, you have to think about what will be best for your videos. It depends on what kind of video it is. Or more specifically, what kind of music video is it? What kind of song and band is it? What genre is it? You aren't going to promote a pop song over a death metal radio station, right? To each, their own. Let's use a rock song for an example. You can promote it over a small radio station; you can make posters and place them inside rock bars and such. But your main weapon will be the internet.

The World Wide Web is a place where one individual can find anything he wants (I mean, you are reading this through the power of the Internet after all). Since the Web is a huge place, I'll be more specific. You Tube, iTunes, Spotify and of course, social networks. Just sharing something can make an impact. You know how it goes, you put it up, your friend sees it, that friend has another friend, that friend has another friend and so on. The beauty of it is, if placed properly, hundreds could see it within minutes, thousands even. And every one of them helps you get to your goal. Keep everything in mind. Post ads on the Internet, make a thread on a forum, and message a band on Facebook, whatever you want.

The band's success also depends on your own so if that band ever gets famous one day, you can be damn sure that they'll remember where they started out and in business terms that means you've got yourself a long-term client.

Another option you might consider is to approach a slightly more established artist and offer to shoot a free video to help build your personal portfolio. Just approaching someone with a bit more renown can be quite stressing and make you uncertain about things, but don't fret too much about it. You've got nothing to lose by asking but if you don't ask, you'll never know of what might have been. Doing a free video might also sound a bit too much but it's for the sake of your future as a filmmaker. One free video to get a higher tier of clients sounds like a pretty good bargain to me. Google a bit and find a few candidates nearby, you can try to e-mail them or contact them over phone, any way works. Either way, the point is to contact them and make your offer.

10. Promoting the video

I told you above, the Internet is your greatest weapon and the best way to promote your videos would probably be You Tube. I mean, it's free and millions frequent it every day so it wouldn't be far-fetched to say that you could succeed with it. I have a few tips for you in order to make your videos more popular.

You need a video that will complement and enhance the song, a video that people will not only watch on repeat, but they'll copy the link and send it over to all of their friends. Make it unique through your ideas and the video will be a bomb.

I said before that the band's success also depends on your success. If your client (the band) wants to become more known out there, you can suggest that they do a cover song. Cover one of the popular mainstream songs and upload it to You Tube, that's one of the surest ways to get new views, especially if it's a good cover.

Be patient. Yes, patience is also a factor here. Fame and renown won't come over night, you know? It will take a great deal of time and effort before you manage to get your name out there. But when you do, it will all be worth it.

Create something relatable. The video should enhance the song and the better you enhance it (but keep it simple, you don't want the video to be complicated to watch), the bigger audience it will get. Everyone's got some problems today and picking out the more frequent ones shouldn't be a problem. Some don't like the government, some are anxious, some are/were bullied, some are depressed, some angry etc. You get the picture. If the video fits the song very well, you'll manage to pull out an emotional reaction in the viewers and that means that you did a good job.

Know your audience. You have to know at which crowd the song is directed at. Is it more of a love song or a rap song? A rock song or heavy metal? I told you before that promoting it everywhere might not be a bad idea but to preserve money and time, target the right ones. You'll have the most success with teenagers because of the diversity within them. Since they're going through puberty and all that, they're more emotional and easy to relate to anything. Film it, post it on You Tube and watch the views climb.

11. Conclusion

We've finally reached the end of our little journey here. I've shown you everything I know and it is up to you to figure out how to use it and mold it into something of your own. You will develop your own style over time, it might be even better than mine (it probably will). Start slowly at first, you don't want to overburden yourself right in the beginning, before you even know how things work. Take one job at a time, no matter how small it is or how small the pay is, it's worth it in the end. Success doesn't come over night, it might not come in a week, month or even a year, but if you stay vigilant, it will come.

There is no greater feeling than that when your hard work gets payed off. This is a risky business and there is no one-hundred percent sure prize or job, you just have to take the risk and make it happen. The majority of the bands you'll encounter at first don't really have any money on them so 'profit' is something you will barely feel. But if you keep going, things will be different later on. A valuable thing to remember while shooting is to have fun, you are doing this because you like it, so don't stress it or anything. Just smile and film it the way you want it. Remember the steps that I told you here. Plan ahead, storyboard it, examine the song and lyrics, find the perfect location and start shooting!

Remember what I asked you at the beginning? Are you willing to do this? Are you still willing to do this after everything you've read up above? Yeah, it's going to be a lot of hard work. Countless hours at the camera, countless hours at your computer, it will pretty much take a lot of time before you feel satisfied with what you do. I've said it before and I'll say it again, IT'S WORTH IT! Besides, you're doing the job you like, see, you're already somewhere better than before. Stay positive and keep on smiling.

I hope this has helped you in any way. If it did help anyone out there, I will be glad it did. Who knows? Maybe you're the next Hitchcock? Anything's possible. We all have to start somewhere and that starting location is our choice. Without further ado, I wish you all the luck in the world and, of course, happy shooting!

FREE Bonus

Book

The Indie Artist Takeover

Why Record Labels Are A Thing of the Past and Indie Artists Are the Future

Table of Contents

Why an Independent Musician No Longer Needs a Record Deal

You have probably heard of the likes of Macklemore & Ryan Lewis, Mumford & Sons and others who have succeeded without the help of a record deal. In the past, many aspiring musicians had the goal of signing a record deal and getting their big break. However, currently, things have changed a lot because now the independent musician is more knowledgeable about the various ways their music career can progress without the help of a record label. It is becoming more evident that musicians no longer need record deals and can actually make it on their own. Further outlined below are reasons why this is so.

The Lack of Authenticity

When it comes to connecting, having an identity and creating a brand, record labels have the tendency of following a formula that is currently obsolete. Their lack of authenticity is evident when they spend millions trying to brand artists in a way that they think will sell the music. In the process, they fail to show the world the real artist, the person behind the music. They fail to notice that showing the world the real person will establish a real connection and that is where the real substance is. When their branding efforts fail and after some time the artist's connection to their fan base fails too, the record label then drops the artist and turns on the next promising artist.

The Useful Social Media Platforms

Many artists are choosing the independent path and have the hope of making it, thanks to the freely available and very convenient social media platforms. Struggling and talented musicians are discovering that the wide range of opportunities for promoting their music can actually help them launch their careers and make their music lucrative. This has made many record labels to become less needed currently by musicians compared to the pre-internet era.

Artists Reap Better Financial Rewards On Their Own

Of course it is an advantage to have the security of a record deal which will channel money into different areas of your music such as promotion, distribution, studio sessions and quality music videos. However, later when you fully understand how the record labels work, it becomes as clear as day that the musicians are not reaping the real financial rewards as they should, the record labels unfortunately do that. Independent musicians have more money going directly to their pockets once their music becomes popular with their fans. There is no cut for the record label and the money only covers the required expenses.

More Artists Are Making It On Their Own

More success stories of musicians who have chosen the independent path are springing up. As long as the musician focuses on creating good music and becoming well-versed with the business aspect of it, they have a great chance of making it independently. Many musicians have realized that and have become successful, something that has provided inspiration to many others who would have otherwise not realized their full potential.

Getting Dropped Without Warning

Many artists who have signed record deals find themselves under immense pressure to perform. They are often times harboring that fear of getting dropped without warning when they cease becoming hits. It doesn't matter if they have an album deal, if they are no longer the next big thing; the record company simply drops them. Who needs to live with that pressure and fear? Most artists prefer to do things on their own without worrying if they are living up to the record label's standards.

The Ugly Fights

It is not uncommon to hear of musicians falling out with their record labels because of royalties or getting dropped without warning. Some have sued each other resulting in a media frenzy and endless drama. Who needs such drama when they can take the independent path and not have to fight over rip-offs, royalties or other mismanagement issues with anyone? Most musicians are trying as much as possible to appear in the public eye as serious artists because of their great music and not because of court cases with major record companies.

Record labels Are Only Interested in Established Musicians

Record labels especially the major ones always turn a blind eye on unproven acts. They don't want to risk anything because they are in business after all. They will never invest thousands or millions of dollars and time on anyone who might not be the real deal. They are always out there looking for musicians who have proven themselves and already have an established market for their music. Most beginning musicians unfortunately fall under the unproven acts category and can't get any record company interested yet. With the availability of social media platforms, musicians don't really need a record deal to help them   get started and besides, they really have no choice but to take the independent path before anyone notices that they actually exist. It is also satisfying for many artists to learn that many major record labels have been turned down by many musicians who are currently successful as independent artists.

More Control for the Musician

Musicians have more control when it comes to the content of their music. They can write songs based on how inspired they feel without anyone directing their flow. This has resulted to great music that fans identify with. Some record deals dictate to their musicians the kind of music they should sing, if they feel that the market needs it. Their interests are purely profit-oriented and some even go as far as hiring songwriters to write music for their musicians to sing. Because the musician has signed a deal, they have no choice but to do the record label's bidding until they are dropped for a better musician of course. It is a business through and through and the record label and not the musician has the helms.

Going the independent path as a musician is not the proverbial walk in the park, but it no doubt gives the artist more control and more peace. More artists are pulling out or contemplating pulling out of major record labels and this is not without reasons. If musicians like Lecrae and the other big names have made it so far independently, any determined musician can make it.

If you are an upcoming artist or talented artist planning to start your music career, then you might have heard of A&R (Artist and Repertoire). When signing up with any recording label, whether big or small, there is need to understand what A&Rs do. Ordinarily, these are people at a record label that are in charge of finding and subsequently developing new talent. They search for the up-and-coming artists and do everything possible to ensure they get the musicians a hit record. When signing up with any record label, the AR person will be responsible for choosing which producer, engineer and studio you will use. They will decide which of your songs can bring in big cash and if you are a great performer but can't write your own music, they always ensure they get you the right materials. The A&R persons can be viewed by different sides of the music industry and can have a positive influence on the upcoming artist's talent or a limitation to the signing career of the artist. If you are an artist with sensibilities on a given genre of music and aims at playing huge stadiums, then a record label A&R can help you join the big league by ensuring your tracks have a commercial edge. To many upcoming singers, their songs are more like a baby, which ideally makes it difficult for them   to discard them   or rather look at them objectively. A good A&R can hence push the artists further in developing their talent and creativity.

Once a single or album recording is complete it is the responsibility of the A&R personnel to get people excited about your music. They distribute your music to retail sales outlets as well as radio stations out there. However, the fierce competition in the music industry has caused artists to have an increasingly short shelf-life. As such, most A&R would want to work with artists who already have a sizeable following before they sign up. With constant touring, self-promotion and getting yourself a good social network following, you'll be on the radar within no time.

Is the A &R era over?

Times are definitely changing with social media now providing artists with an ideal platform for promoting their music without the push of major record labels and most upcoming artists have actually found out that they can make it on their own. With social media tools like Twitter, Instagram, YouTube, and SoundCloud, upcoming artists can upload their music and have it reach a much wider audience compared to the times when social media wasn't there. Marketing music on the social media can even get an artist a solid fan base which ideally doesn't require the artist to sign up with a famous record label in order to have his or her music get any airplays and even top the charts.

Even though famous labels and imprints are not needed that much as they were during the pre-internet era, they are undeniably doing a great job in pumping money into major areas like distribution, promotion, organizing studio sessions and doing music videos. The record label's aim   is to ensure the artist's music comes out with great quality and that a wider audience gets to know about the new artist's recorded music. The record label the artist is working with will generate the much-needed revenue from   the artist's songs and the profits will be shared on a given percentage as agreed in the sign up contract. However, when you look keenly into the inner working so the major record labels plus the contracts the upcoming artists sign, you'll discover the musicians are not actually reaping the financial rewards from   their talent. While you might be under the assumption that you can never make it in the music industry without the backing of a major record label, you can be surprised how you can hit the charts as an independent artist working with an independent label. All you need to do is utilize social media, make good music and have a good funding for your music recording. You don't really need to sign up with a label or make any deal.

You're Already Your Own A&R (artist & repertoire)

Becoming an independent artist is what most upcoming artists are opting for and this ultimately means money from   the sales and distribution directly goes into their pockets. Arguments still persist in the major record labels over royalties and the fear of being dropped without warning. Despite signing to a multi-single or album   deal, upcoming artists still find it a challenge working with the major music labels. Currently, most upcoming artists are not willing to have the major labels take control of the promotion when they (artists) have social at their disposal to reach their fans directly. They can independently record their songs, upload the music to YouTube or SoundCloud and get the desired plays that will make them   famous and also pump in the cash from   the plays.

Working as an independent artist while utilizing the social media to market your music doesn't mean you won't get any challenges. Considering the instant nature of promoting music through social media tools like YouTube Twitter, Instagram or SoundCloud, you'll discover that many artists are actually overselling and exposing themselves too quickly before they can build upon experience. While it's ordinarily necessary to have a record label amplify your art, you can still take the risk of walking into the unknown by working as an independent artist. When you sign to an independent label, you as an artist will have more control in your music career in terms of creativity and the financial aspect as well.

The role of the major record labels might be seen to be more of a multiple service provider. They ideally offer investment and marketing for artists that have already gained modest to medium success while working on their own but would want to make a greater impact on their music career. For artists who are still budding, there are labels, publishers and managers who are willing to work with new artists through investing a significant amount of time and money. But even with unlimited funds to get started, you as an upcoming artist can get into the limelight by promoting your music on the major social media platforms. With good quality music, you can reach more and more fans on the social media platform and makes significant proceeds from their music without really breaking a sweat.it isn't really necessary that you attach yourself to a famous recording label in order for you to realize success in the music industry.

Who Needs a Record Label When You Can Press Up Your Own CD's, Vinyl Records, Cassette Tapes, Download Cards, and DVD'S?

When you're trying to become a musician, your goal is always to make sure you come off as professional. When you work with a distributor or some kind of label, you kind of have them to give you pointers, but there are many benefits to going at this all on your own. They may give you great suggestions and tips, but usually they could control everything else about your music. Going into this alone and selling your music as an individual may seem   tough, but there are countless opportunities for serious growth and learning. The key is to remember that research and knowledge go a long way.

Most musicians when they're starting out usually have the music ready, and they are oftentimes prepared for having their music sell on iTunes and even sell independently in stores. However, the toughest part is just knowing what to do with CDs, covers, download cards, and all the other promotional materials to promote your music and make sure you're showcased as a professional.

Believe it or not, you can actually get all of these things made for a good price on the web. Almost everything and anything can be made for you even if you don't have all the connections when you look at the Internet. Getting into the music industry is hard in itself, and so there are definitely hurdles to overcome when going at it alone, but one thing that can be done fairly easy even for novice musicians is getting all the material made.

Let's start with CDs first since it's CDs most musicians get started off with:

When it comes down to CDs, you can press them   all on your own. You have about two options when going at this alone: you can do it yourself with a couple of minimal equipment or you can just hire a company to do it for you.

- Press Your CDs by Yourself

To do it on your own, you'll need to have the CDs ready for the work involved. You need to have the blank CDs ready in hand and a computer. That's ready it. You will need a printer, of course, to print out a cover for the CD. Don't forget about the CD cases. Of course, while this is a bit tough to do and a bit timely, it's your best bet if you are on a budget.

You'll need to have the music all on your computer ready for download. I sent the blank disk and copy the music onto the CD. Don't forget to use audio CDS instead of data CDs since they don't play on all CD players. Different computers will be either slower or faster when uploading to a CD, but it shouldn't take too long. After a while, you should be able to have the music on multiple CDs. With the covers printed, you'll be ready for selling these CDs in no time.

You will find that there are countless sites online that will do this tedious task for you. Working with a professional company can give your CDs a quick extra spark in the quality of the covers and also in the music. You can be sure that every CD turns out well and plays the music correctly. You can work with sites like CDPressing.com or CDPrintExpress.com.

Download Cards

Download cards are great for getting your music out there. It's a great marketing tool for advertising your music in the most unique way possible outside of the online world. These can be on your very own, but buying them on the web like on websites like FizzKicks.com could be a better option because of their amazing design opportunities and options for getting the perfect download card. The reason why download cards work so well is that they're so traditional. Making music online is definitely the way to go, especially since social media is where to be if you want to make it in music. However, going the traditional route and getting people in your area to listen to your music, watch a gig of yours, or simply check out your website can go a long way for getting your music out there.

Download cards could simply tell people about your upcoming CD being released or a show you're going to have. Believe it or not, you could get a lot of people heading to your website this way as well. If you use a unique way of convincing people to check out your site or iTunes page, you could achieve a lot of attention just be putting yourself out there. Download cards are also very affordable. It is highly recommended that when you get the made professionally that you use them   for a multi-purpose thing down the road. It would be a waste if you bought it advertising a one-time event. You want it to sell a song of yours that they would buy down the road.

These all can be done with a professional company, but doing them on your own is also an option. Obviously, not all of you are going to try and create cassette tapes or vinyl records, but it can all be done. Just a quick set of basic research could allow for you to get these things made for you if you wanted.

To succeed in the world of music, you need to be very knowledgeable and prepared to put in the work. Promoting is a huge thing you need to do in order to get your music out there. When it comes down to getting your CDs ready, both options of going either free or paid can be worth doing. Just look at your budget to see what may work best for you. Creativity alone goes a long way. If you're on a budget, doing it all alone can easily be a great option for the long haul to save cash.

Who Needs a Record Label When You Can Get Your Music on iTunes By Yourself?

Whether you have a band or you're a solo artist, you'll find that getting your music out there is not that easy. Trying to distribute your music and getting your name out there is not always a simple task. Most musicians seek out a distributor to get their music into stores. But the truth is you do not need them to get your music out there. Selling your own music via iTunes is not only a possibility, but it's a real way to get started without needing to make huge connections with other people. Discover in this specific section how to get your music on iTunes.

Can You Sell Your Own Music via iTunes Yourself?

Absolutely yes. It's a great way to get on the right track without having to get yourself in front of music producers. Getting any kind of label or distributor is extremely tough when you're getting started. Investing in professional recording work, time in a recording studio, album covers, cd creation, and paying for a demo is all very much required in order to be recognized and picked up by a label. When you go independent, you have a better shot at just getting your feet wet in the industry. You can just get your music made in your own home, and then add it to the iTunes system. Of course, you'll be getting a quick run through on how to do that in this section, but I want you to know that you do not need to invest in a demo to get yourself out there.

For a lot of musicians today, songwriting has played a huge role for their success. It is not uncommon in today's world for some people to write their own songs and sell it. Taylor Swift, for example, has inspired millions of young musicians to create their own music. With the songwriting skill and a bit of instrumental knowledge, it's quite possible for anybody with the determination to create a beautiful song and a great EP to begin with.

You'll find that most people will still try to go after finding a record label or find a distributor simply because they believe it's the only way in the industry. It's still an effective way to succeed, but it definitely is not the only way available. If you want to get into the music industry, here is a quick outline to get your music on iTunes.

- Get Your Music Made First

Whether it's a single or a full album   that you would like to sell, you need to just get it made. Just get it all organized, recorded, edited, and then ready for the iTunes world. Now, you don't think you're just going to pay some small fee and then put it up on their iTunes Store. It doesn't work like that.

- Apple Has High Expectations

In order to sell a song on iTunes straight from   the site, they expect that you have created 20 albums and all kinds of stuff before distribution that can hinder everything. You need to have a high level of previous success to go straight into their database of musicians. So how do you get on iTunes, you may ask? It's all very simple and quite easy to understand.

- Apple Has Created Smaller Options

The best part about the iTunes Store is that you can put your music in front of thousands of people without having to reach their high expectations. With companies like TuneCore, you could submit your music through them   to get on iTunes. They have membership options to be able to choose for your specific goals and what you want to do with your songs. You can choose their "single" option that lets you sell your single for less than $10. It's really cheap to work with them. They have specific conditions you must apply and understand, but they are very lenient.

There are other sites and companies that do the same as TuneCore. They all work in a very similar fashion. They connect you to the iTunes Store, and they simply work with you so that your music is sellable and is ready for the sales. They also work diligently with iTunes so that you get the money you deserve. There are price cuts, but TuneCore does not take any royalties. They just connect you with iTunes. They have specific pricing plans for you to use to decide on the kind of different music you want to put up for sale on the iTunes Store.

CD BABY is another good option you will find to be available. There are countless people who find this to be a bit more expensive. But they do have great options. Either site provides you with similar chances to get in the iTunes marketplace.

Promotion Is Vital

A song being put on the iTunes does not mean anything without proper marketing and advertising. The songs you put up on iTunes must really be promoted on any other social media you may have. Promoting a song is tough, but properly getting your name out there and building a following is something you can work on right at this moment.

Do not forget to get that cover photo made for your iTunes song. You need to be ready musically and also in terms of showing your presence to everybody. It'll be a lot easier in the long run when you go this way and have everything prepared.

Do you still need a distributor? There are I any people who will still look for a distributor, but it's not always needed. With resources like TuneCore, you don't need to work with anybody but yourself. Just a little tiny upfront investment into their system, and you'll be on your way to succeeding with selling your own music. Selling your music via your own means is so much easier knowing that you have complete control of your creative musical side. With complete control, you can stick to the music you want to make.

Benefits of Setting Up A Home Studio

For years, the music industry has failed to provide musicians with the services that they deserve. Right from   the contracts artists have to sign, to the recording stage down to selling the music, musicians have for long felt that they are not getting the share that they have worked so hard for and rightfully deserve. As a result, most musicians have contemplated going independent, rather that signing with record labels and it has proved to be a wise decision to make. One of the steps to take towards becoming an independent musician is establishing your own state-of-the-art home studio. Provided you get the right equipment and you possess the skills, you will be surprised that home studios can produce sound quality just as good as professional recording studios.

Always Have A plan

The first step will be coming up with a viable plan for the new home studio. Before you start recording, always have a pre-production to test the quality of your equipment and skills. You need to craft out the sounds, effects, harmonies and the alternate chords so that you determine what will go where. A dummy track will help you in outlining the plan. All you have to do is record a demo and then create a few other mixes, some without drums, bass and other components of the beat. By the time you come up with the full version, you will be well conversant with the new equipment.

Have a Conducive Working Environment

When producing your own music, creating a comfortable working space is important so that productivity is at its peak. Your creativity in production increases if you have all hats you need around your desk. The room   should not be congested and stuffy as this will limit your ability to work according to your full potential. You should also have a team   that assists you with the production since certain areas require skills that you may not possess. This way, your home studio will be nothing short of what you are used to at the professional studio.

A home studio has several advantages that you don't enjoy at the professional studios. As your own boss, your level of commitment and discipline will be at a whole new level as you will be responsible for your own success or failure. Since you will also fear to see your investment go down the drain, you will always be at your best. The other advantages include:

Convenience

When going to a professional studio to rehearse, artists and band members have to carry all their musical instruments with them. These hassles won't be there if you have a home studio since you will have your equipment within reach, whenever you need them. This is very convenient for you and you can always work on your vocals and practice from the comfort of your home.

Time Flexibility

In the professional studios, you always have to work on rigid time periods which are pre-determined by your producer. Working on scheduled appointments which don't factor in time for personal and other activities is difficult. Sparing a room in your home for a studio provides you with time flexibility and you can always get down to work whenever it is convenient for you.

Cost Effective

Producing your music in a professional studio is an expensive affair. You will have to part with a lot of money and at the same time, your returns will not be as rewarding. This is not value for your money as you are charged by the hour. If you have your own home studio, you can practice with ease without any hurry and you don't have to feel pressured every time the clock ticks. The only cost you incur is the initial cost of purchasing the equipment and the normal maintenance expenditure. You can spend as much time as you wish in the studio practicing and recording. Basically, you get everything you can find in the professional studio, but minus the cost.

Innovation and creativity

Hiring someone to produce your music limits your creativity as you won't have much say in what goes on in the production end, but you will focus only on composing and singing. Moreover, most of the music we hear nowadays is a product of music recorded, mixed and mastered at home. At your home studio, you can try out anything you think will make your music great, meaning that you will be highly innovative than when in a professional studio.

Better Quality

The calm ambiance of a home studio makes a musician be in the right emotional and mental state to come up with top-notch final product. Everything is self-paced without any hurry and pressure and your productivity will be off the roof. Similarly, having the privilege to listen to any mistakes and errors you may make gives you an opportunity to sharpen your skills. This gives you room for improvement, self-growth and you can take your abilities to the next level.

Choice of Equipment

When you go to a professional studio, you can only work with what is provided to you. The producer will only purchase the equipment that he sees necessary and your preference is none of their worries. When running your own home studio, you can determine the musical instruments that will best suit your needs for better output. Obviously, you will purchase all your favorite instruments that you can get your hands on and your recording ventures will be exactly what you wish for.

Make Some Extra Cash

Apart from   the above benefits, a home studio is a smart investment and you can use it to make money. You can always rent it out to interested parties and charge them   per hour as you make some useful extra income. You don't lose anything as you will be producing your own music at a lower cost and help others minimize cost as you earn from   the opportunity.

At the end of the day, you will produce even better music from your home studio than you can in a professional studio. In addition to high-quality music, you also benefit from   the numerous advantages as discussed.

You're already marketing yourself as an artist

To become famous and successful in the music industry really requires perfect organization of oneself as a musician. The key point here is how you express yourself to the public or the audience which will make them   make a positive judgment about you. Many musicians are still struggling and even other have ended up quitting this music industry because of lack of proper expression to the audience. On the other hand, various musicians are very popular to the public and they really enjoy themselves as being part of the music industry. This is because they took the proper approach to their audience.

The way a musician expresses himself/herself to the public depends on many reasons which have influence on the success of a music business. This is perfectly understood by considering the points discussed below.

Being committed

This consists of two decisions;

Acknowledging that you are the only one responsible for the success of your music business because you have the capability to do what you want.

Recognizing that every decision you make is either taking you close to your music business goals or it is taking you away from it.

By fast failing or often failing

Doing something so fast might cause you to crash on the way. Though most of the time when you are extremely ambitious in achieving your plans, provided you have the right decision to "go pro" and you have a strong foundation to work from then you will not crash. Instead, you will only discover that you are able to work faster, harder, and longer than once you thought before. This is every time you are going for something using the past experience you will be expanding the capacity of handling the prevailing situation. Failure should be embraced as it helps you to learn what doesn't work. The only way to know if you are pushing harder enough is through failing which in turn aids you to learn the best ways to handle a situation.

Be or Do a Little Better

To make money in the music business does have to be necessarily a lot better than your fellow musicians, you just have to be a little better and you will notice the difference automatically. Comfort is the main enemy the ruins excellence. This is because the more successful and older we get, the more we become comfortable and stop going for more. The key to long-term improvement and to become consistent is by doing it slowly and gradually.

Qualities you should have:

These are all essential for the success of your music business.

Ability to make a wise decision. This will make you become motivated fast and will, therefore, increase your hustle. This will enable you to look for opportunities to make money through your music business from different acts whether teaching lessons, scoring films or playing weddings.

Having knowledge of your destination. It involves knowing what is essential for the success of your business. This is because it will give you a reference point where you work from. It depends on other factors such as dreaming big, asking yourself what you want for your success, and being focused.

Flexibility and Openness. Normally, people change, opportunities change and plans change. This is one of the best reasons why you should be flexible to review to set goals every time you find new opportunities. This means that you should not keep your things shut instead try to add something better which will keep options of your end goal to be open.

Ability to start something even when you are afraid.
Normally there is no perfect time to work on anything. This means that you should not worry to try doing something just because you don't know much about it. Instead, you have to start because out there in the field is where you will learn many things.

Ability to manage your time. You should focus on tasks because this will add the value of your music and brand in a way that is both measurable and specific. This means you can focus on tasks that will earn you money (such as selling of albums) or those that will get you in front of your audience (such as playing shows).

Business and Personal Support. Business support is those people whom you can call them to offer business support or to answer a business-related question. Personal support is a group of people outside the business and they are able to give perspective or advice you on non-business issues.

Supportive infrastructure. This involves many things that affect the successful of your music business. These include the things you should do to make you function properly, what you should eat, the things you should away from, and how much sleep you need. Apart from these things there are others like the type of transportation you require to conduct your business, where you need to live, and the skills you need to have to make you succeed.

Distraction management. You can easily spot distractions related to other people but noticing distractions related to oneself is much difficult. Check on how you spend your time, resources, and energy. This will help you in discovering the distractions that stop you from moving forward.

It doesn't have to be so perfect. At one time, you could feel as if what you are doing is not perfect top your fans but that should not worry you, just believe in what you do and always aim higher.

Build an audience. When you have decided to build your career in the music business, then the best recommendation is to get committed to building your audience. This is because when you are committed to giving them   what they need they will also commit themselves to you. Normally every musician who stays in the music business for long has that capability to create a strong audience. These can be done by applying the following rules; respect, love, and give your audience the value they want.

Expressing yourself to the public will have an effect on your work as a musician. Success in music business needs you to overcome your fears and make it happen. Be clear on what you want and chase after it with everything you have got.

You Already Promote Yourself via Social Media

Back in the 90's or even the early 2000's, it would require extreme promotional efforts to reach some kind of audience. Radio tours, local concerts, and countless marketing tactics are needed in order to get the attention, but in today's generation, building a following has become a thousand times easier. If you have ever used a social media site or app, then you have already utilized the resource for building your following.

Social media has changed the lives of countless musicians. With singers like Shawn Mendes, Tori Kelly, and even Pentatonix, who has built their following through their social media, they have become practically household names in the world of music from   social media.

Building A Following Has Never Been Easier With The Internet And Social Networks

Believe it or not, there's more to the Internet than your typical social media sites. There are special apps and social networking sites that have built the careers of countless musicians. You're already using the right networks on a daily basis, so you might as well use it to promote yourself. Sadly, gone are the days where you can post a cover on YouTube and you could expect thousands of it views right off the bat. To build a following, you need to do more than just posting a video. Today, I'll be giving you what you need to get on the right path.

What Social Networks Can Really Build My Career?

Today, there are more than enough you could access online. While YouTube is the place to be, there are still so many opportunities to succeed without using just that site. We all know that YouTube is extremely popular, but it's filled with tons of other artists. You should still continue posting videos, building your subscribers, and also connecting and collaborating with other artists. However, you need to venture out of that to see true and fast success. You need to work hard at promoting yourself, but with the right tricks, you'll be on your way to social media growth.

- Soundcloud

If you're a singer ready to get a following, start posting your original songs and cover on Soundcloud. This website is focused primarily for musicians trying to bring their voices to the web. The reason why it's so successful is because it allows musicians to let listeners and potential future fans to hear just the music itself without letting looks get in the way. You need to start posting on Soundcloud. It's best to post covers, but once you get your followers, you can promote almost everything and anything to them   to buy your song.

- Twitter, Instagram, And Facebook

These three social networks are considered the "power 3". These three social networks are not exactly the networks that will get you the following for your music. However, you will still need to use these to help create the quality of your online presence. With an Instagram   account, you can showcase videos and also show your daily life. Facebook fan pages are also great for showing your brand, your music, and making updates with your music. The same goes for your Twitter account. These three are still great for just building a brand.

- Vine

In the world of music today, Vine has become a HUGE social network. It is from   this app alone that built the careers of singers like Shawn Mendes and singing groups like Us The Duo. Both musical acts started out singing on Vine and sharing their voices with the 6-second video. The idea behind

Vine is that it only allows you to share videos that are only 6 seconds long. This forces people to become increasingly creative right away. That isn't easy to do. When you perfect your style of music and you know how to stand out in your Vine videos, you'll be able to grab people and get their attention.

As a singer, you too could post videos on this app. Building a following is much easier on this app because you aren't competing against hundreds of thousands of other musical hopefuls. It's tough to build a following on sites like YouTube because of all the competition, but Vine is still an open place to get a following.

Tips On Using Vine

The best tip to remember why using Vine is that you shouldn't blatantly promote anything just yet. Build a following. Lead people to your SoundCloud covers if you'd like. Just make it a goal to provide great singing in 6 seconds. It allows you to actually provide short teasers to make people want more from you. To build a following, providing great covers of famous songs is important, but be sure to watch out for big Vine musicians. Some of them   with hundreds of thousands of followers may be willing to share your Vines, causing you to get more followers and views, or, in this case, loops. As a Vine is played, it loops on its own. Make remakes of other Viners you're a fan of and they just might share your Vine out to their followers and revine it.

Outside of those social networks, there are all kinds of things to help build your brand as a musician. The truth about musicians is that you can build a career from the bottom up on social media sites alone. With the proper understanding on promoting yourself, you'll get yourself out there easier. The truth about the world of music today is that you don't need to go the traditional route. You can go your own way on the web. Every single potential fan of yours is on the web and other famous apps right now. If you reach out to them and get yourself out in front of them, they'll become a fan of yours.

Think of the world of social media as a powerful source for building a serious fan base simply because it truly can get you followers. You may not know how powerful using Soundcloud, Vine, a bit of YouTube, and of course Twitter, Instagram, and Facebook can be for building your brand. You'll be building a following and creating a fan base that will soon enough buy your music.

Crowdfunding: Why You Need to Embrace it if You're a Musician

Judging from the current state of the music industry, it's safe to say that artists no longer need record labels to hit a home run. Nowadays, taking a cue from artists such Pomplamoose and Amanda Palmer, artists can take the DIY route and still run their music as a business.

Gone are the days when money was considered an issue for a budding musician or the main reason many artists found it safe to tie themselves up to a record label. Today, artists have a thousand and one ways to creatively finance their own tours and albums, with the most viable option being crowdfunding.

Crowdfunding is a very valuable money generating tool that hard up artists can leverage to fund their projects. It's a strategy that has worked for many artists not subsisting on label money.

The best part about crowdfunding is that, if done correctly, it has more to offer to a dedicated, creative artist than just money. Besides helping you raise oodles of money, it's a good platform   to connect with your fans on a whole new level and create an unbreakable bond.

But there's more to it than the fantasy you've been trying to create in your head. Not everyone will be flat out jacked about your idea to make a pledge and share it around.

There's a fair chance that things may NOT turn out like envisioned if you do not bring your thoughts together and come up with a proper plan and strategy.

Why Should You Embrace Crowdfunding?

To have 100 percent ownership of your music

You've put an all-out effort perfecting your piece, burning the mid-night oil practicing and cramming your lyrics, you deserve total ownership of your music and everything that comes out of it.

With crowdfunding, you get to keep everything earned without being forced to give account to anyone. Musicians such Jen Cloher and Sam Buckingham are a living proof of what crowdfunding can do to level up the playing ground of a budding artist who's strapped for cash without cheating them out of ownership.

Use Crowdfunding to Stay Out Of Debt

Every now and then you keep hearing about signed artists declaring bankruptcy to get out debts. That's an ungodly rabbit hole you don't want to get in for sure.

You shouldn't take this path when you can sell your music and tickets via crowdfunding to get your projects off the ground without risking running into debts.

Many people against the idea of crowdfunding say it's tantamount to begging fans for money. But in reality, crowdfunding is more like preselling your project, tickets, and album. It's a win-win situation for both the supporter and musician—the musician gets the funding, the fan gets to enjoy the first dibs that come out of the project.

More Opportunities

Crowdfunding has turned out to be much more than a great platform   for funding a project. For one, the platform   features all types of people in the music industry running the gamut from   other artists and music producers to event organizers and media influencers.

A case in point, the April Maze Folk duo while carrying out their crowdfunding business on Kickstarter were introduced Hannah Acfield, who started touring with them   exposing their music to a whole new audience.

A number of projects have managed to attract additional funding from   councils and grant bodies after their campaigns ended. Because, for one, a successful campaign can be a good proof that you already have an audience for your project. This is particularly essential if you're hoping to start your own label someday and are looking for investors to go in with you.

How to make people pledge to your project

. – Assure them that that's your best work ever

Your fans will be quick to chip in and pledge if you assure them that you're working on something that outstrips all your previous work. Use words such as "AWESOME" while describing the project. Then proceed to give details on what exactly gives the project wings.

. – Make the project appear like a great opportunity you wouldn't want to pass

Take your time to explain your current situation to your fans. Tell them how you've always wished to work with a certain big producer or go on tour with a certain band then go ahead to tell them that this project is the only thing that makes that dream a possibility. Should the project flop then you don't stand another chance of seeing that dream come true.

. – Make your fans part of the project

Your fans should be like an extension of you. If they like your music, they'll pretty much want you to succeed the same way you wish yourself success.

So don't deny them the opportunity to be part of your success. And the only way to do this is to make them part of your project and team.

Ask them to be "part of your BIG project." You can do this by using keywords such as "that's where you come in" or "together, let's make this dream a reality."

. – Remind them of how their contribution makes the project even better

The more people you get to contribute and participate, the more successful your project becomes. So, break the budget into small chunks, starting with the smallest that though won't make the project exemplary, can help get one or two things done.

. – Reward Your Fans

Only a few people have the heart to give something without expecting anything in return. There's a fair chance such people may NEVER get a chance to come across your campaign, but you have the other group to leverage on.

Just come up with something that balances off an exchange. And the best way to do this is to offer free albums, tickets or even an opportunity for a fan to meet and hang out with you if they donate a certain threshold.

Make it known that the rewards are only a prerogative of those willing to pledge generously. And that you'd like to meet them up so you can get to thank them   in person.

Why would People want to Pledge to your Campaign?

Before you even think of pitching your proposal, it's important to ask yourself about what exactly will make your fans want to pledge towards your project.

Among the possible reasons you're likely to come up with, here are the three major reasons why people pledge to a music project:

. – If they're your strong fans, they'll feel obligated to you. They'll feel like it's their responsibility to make things work for you.

. – Others would simply want to support you as an individual. Maybe you remind them   of something or they're just happy to help someone succeed.

. – A good number will pledge because of the personal connection the project creates between the two of you. After all that's the only opportunity they have to connect with you. So they'll want to donate to jumpstart an interaction.

. – As for the rest, it'll be about the perks. They'll do it to get your T-shirts, CDs, customized USBs and all you have to offer. Just make the perks more alluring and you'll have them peppering your donation box with different amounts.

You Can Book Your Own Shows and Tours

It is a huge decision, you have a band, you are doing well, your gigs are getting bigger, your YouTube hits are growing, and you are getting rave reviews, so where to next? You can book your own shows and tours and stay independent, using the ever-increasing on-line channels to promote awareness and get your music out there or approach a record label and try for the big time?

Let's be honest, if you have a mind-boggling act, producing music that is blowing people away you are likely to have agents knocking at the door, good vibes travel fast. However this is rare, it is reputed that the major labels only make a profit out of one in every ten signings. The reality is; you will have lots of competition and the agents and record labels will have lots of choices. You need experience, you need the best material and that takes time and dedication.

Staying independent will afford you more freedom and control of your destiny. You can continue to book your own shows and tours and remain independent, building up a strong fan base. In reality, the process of the 'big time' is likely to be slow but you will remain in charge of the pace and direction of your music. If music is your passion and not the dream of stardom and fame, well this may well be the right course for now.

It is a gamble though, time is money, you need exposure and the right coverage to start making a name and that means lots of recognition. Promoting yourself means playing bigger gigs, building up the fan base and breaking borders to get heard far and wide. You will need to produce quality videos to promote on YouTube and other streaming channels. It means bankrolling your endeavors without the luxury of advance payments, but it does mean the probability of avoiding building up debts. Of course, the more successful you become independently, the better the deal you could strike at a later stage.

Signing to a major record label off course has the promise of quicker success and the backing and expertise to make it all happen. The signing with a major record label will likely seal you anything from 10% - 16% royalties, however, these payments will be made after expenses which can include a host of items from recording, video production, tour, marketing and promotional costs.

The advantages can be major though. Most aspiring musicians want to be signed to have the opportunity to hit the big time. By signing with a major record label, you are investing the band's future in a team of professional experts to help pave the way to success for you and your music. Major record labels offer an experienced team to market and promote your music to the masses through their connections with radio stations, PR stunts and let's be frank, other outlets where one needs contacts.

But you would not be booking your own shows and tours anymore, that freedom along with much more will in all probability be signed away. In reality, a record label will expect and ensure that they do their best to improve their chances of recouping their investment. They will expect and negotiate hard to get the best deal which may well include rights on future albums, promotional material and having all their upfront expenses repaid prior to any royalty payments being disbursed. You need to sign any deal or arrangement being fully aware of all the expectations and clauses in the contract.

Independent labels are a good approach as you can often negotiate a better deal. Although they will not have the same power to distribute and promote your material as the major record labels, you will, however, have more freedom   and possibly be able to drive a better deal. Some independent labels may also provide the opportunity to enable them   to distribute through a major label giving you additional resource when your music reaches the big time, the advantage being that your contract remains with the independent label affording you more creative license and additional freedom.

When signing a contract, you should seek sound legal advice. You cannot negotiate or change details after you have signed the deal, so make sure you are happy with your contract. The time to negotiate is when you get the contract, remember you are entering into what is likely to be a long-term arrangement, make sure everyone is content with the deal. Remember you are at the table because they want to sign you.

Off course going it alone is the option that many artists are pursuing. With good music and self - funding your own label, coupled with social media, the chances of success are more promising than ever. But it will take hard work and you will need to learn along the way. The Association of Independent Music (AIM) provides a platform   for independent musicians to get advice and assistance in setting up an independent label.

What is most important is that you agree your aims and promote your music at every turn. One lucky break, one supporting act and you could be well on your way to stardom. Keep finding innovative ways to interact with your fan base, keep putting fresh and intriguing material on the social networks and work your gigs, every fan counts! The bigger you develop yourselves, the more experience you gain, the better your prospects of securing that lucrative deal.

If your love is the music, producing and performing your passion and you are content with building your fan base steadily; then remain focused on delivering the best music. You can continue book your own shows and tours if you stay independent, growth will inevitably be slower, but you will be in charge of your destiny. Good news travels fast, an agent or record label is sure to spot you and then you are in a better position to negotiate a better deal. Just be sure you get what you want!

You Can License Your Music to TV and Film

Music is one of the most profitable industries in the entertainment business. This is partially because of the demand to license music. Whether it is a local, commercial, or a big budget feature film, almost everything needs music in the background to provide energy and atmosphere. Because of the high demand for music, it is a prime time for musicians, composers, producers, and others with an interest in a career in music to launch their own music publishing company. For composers and songwriters, owning your music publishing company and licensing your own music can be very beneficial. It gives you more control over the copyright ownership and the use of your music than you would have by signing with another third party music publishing company. Although it seems like it could be a difficult process, establishing your own publishing company and licensing your music to television and film for additional income is possible in just a few steps.

The first step in creating your own music publishing company is creating a business and filing it with your state government.

This typically involves an application process and paying a small fee. You can choose to register your new company in a number of different ways including as a limited liability company or a corporation. Some companies also choose to register themselves under a fictitious name with the Secretary of State. Doing this will grant you the right to conduct business under a name other than your full legal name. You must register your company with the government in some way in order for it to operate legally and be taxed properly. This is a crucial step in establishing your music publishing company. Visit https://www.sba.gov to find additional information on getting this process started. In addition to establishing your publishing company, you should also visit a bank and create a business account for your newly registered company.

Once your company has been registered with the government and is an official legal business entity, you should affiliate it with either Broadcast Music Incorporated (also known as BMI) at http://www.bmi.com or ASCAP (also known as the American Society of Composers, Authors, and Publishers) at http://www.ascap.com. Both BMI and ASCAP are performance rights organizations that help to monitor the live and recorded performances of their members, collect the appropriate licensing fees, and distribute these fees to their members. Your company will need to be affiliated with one of these organizations in order to help keep track of your company's songs and make sure you are being properly paid for their use. BMI requires a one-time application fee to be one of their affiliated publishers, while ASCAP bills their affiliated publishers an annual fee. In order to be able to register with BMI or ASCAP, your music must meet one of the following criteria:

- your company must have released a song commercially
- a film is being released that features one of your songs
- a television episode is being released featuring one of your songs
- one of your songs has been broadcasted over the radio

In order to begin your business, your company should own the rights to at least one song that is in the process of or has already been licensed.

The third, and perhaps most important, step for creating your own music publishing company is to create or collect a catalog of songs. Musicians can do this by writing their own music and others interested in music publishing can do this by finding talented artists and buying the rights to some of their songs. Some companies create relationships with songwriters, musicians, and composers and work with clients to create custom songs and scores for their clients. Your company's catalog of songs will be the source of all of its income.

Before you begin actively licensing out your company's music, you should also gain a solid knowledge of the different types of music licenses. There are two main different types of music licenses: mechanical and synchronized licenses. Mechanical licenses authorize a recording label, company, producer, or recording artist to record and distribute a song. A synchronized music license usually pertains to film, television, commercials, and radio in which a song is synchronized to another audio or visual production. You should also be familiar with the rights of copyright owners. For example, copyright owners have the exclusive right to grant permission to other musicians or recording artists to either perform their music live, or record their music for reproduction.

After you have created or collected a sufficient number of songs, you should make sure that they are all registered with the United States Copyright office and either BMI or ASCAP, whichever you affiliated your company with. The performance rights organization you are affiliated with will help you monitor your music to make sure that no one is using them without your permission. The United States Copyright office will help you establish and confirm that your songs belong to you in case someone should try to steal or copy your music.

Once your music has been registered, you now need to work to network and meet music supervisors and music coordinators in the television, commercial, and film industries. Music supervisors and music coordinators are the people responsible for selecting which music their show, commercial, or movie licenses for its use. These types of connections are vital for the success of your company as their licenses will be one of the main sources of income for your company. To successfully license your company's music, you should familiarize yourself with the writer's and publisher's clearance forms of your performance rights organization. This will help either BMI or ASCAP monitor your music's use, keep track of what percentage of revenue to pay the writers and publishers, and know where to send these revenue checks.

Another source of revenue could be licensing out the songs your company owns the rights to. By owning the rights to the intellectual property of the songs itself, you can collect money when another artist records or performs one of your company's songs. This can be a lucrative source of income if your company owns the rights to popular songs or has connections to other popular musicians and recording artists.

Thank you for reading *The Indie Artist Takeover*. We hope that you have found this information useful, and wish you much success on your music journey!

13512089R00060

Printed in Poland
by Amazon Fulfillment
Poland Sp. z o.o., Wrocław